INDIANS OF THE PLAINS

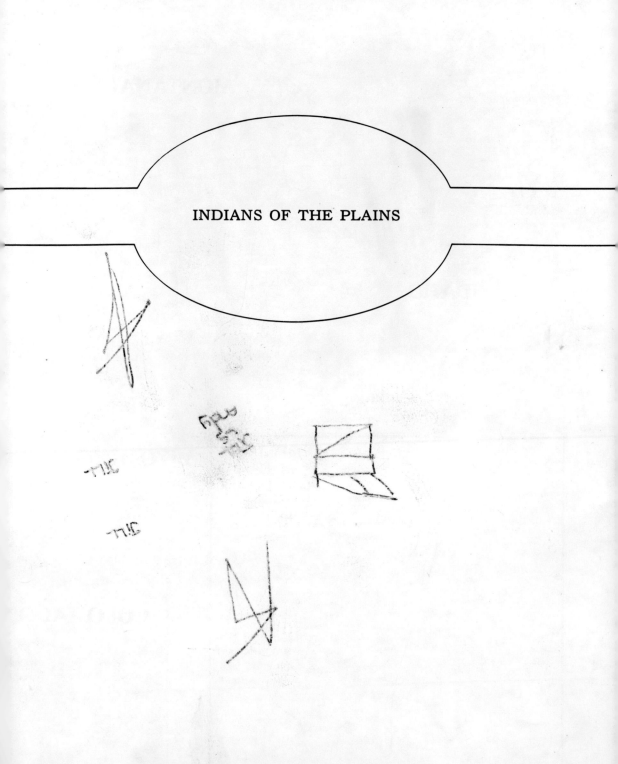

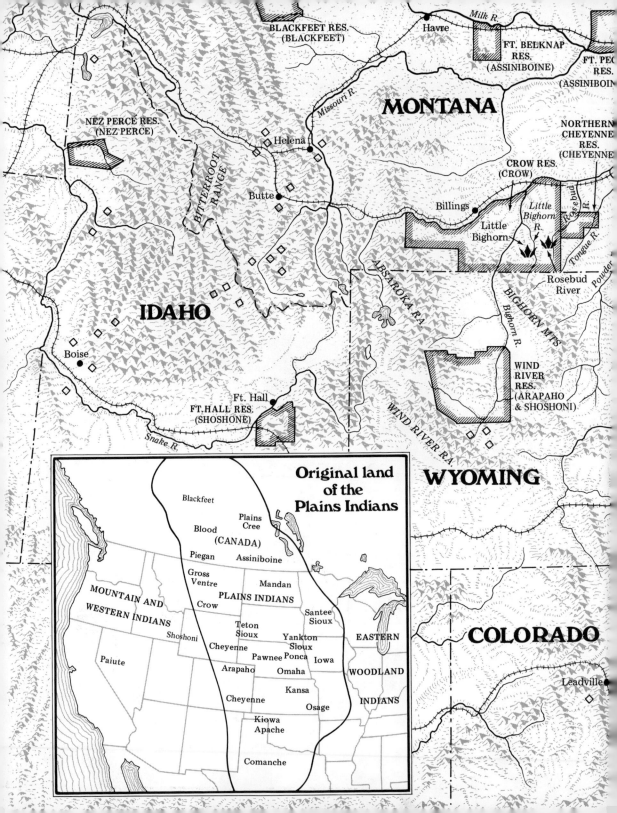

BLACKFEET RES.
(BLACKFEET)

Milk R.

Havre

FT. BELKNAP
RES.
(ASSINIBOINE)

FT. PEC
RES.
(ASSINIBOIN

Missouri R.

MONTANA

NEZ PERCE RES.
(NEZ PERCE)

NORTHERN
CHEYENNE
RES.
(CHEYENNE

Helena

CROW RES.
(CROW)

BITTERROOT RANGE

Rosebud R.

Butte

Billings

Little
Bighorn
R.

Little
Bighorn

Tongue R.

Rosebud
River

Powder

IDAHO

ABSAROKA R.A.

BIGHORN MTS

Bighorn R.

Boise

WIND
RIVER
RES.
(ARAPAHO
& SHOSHONI)

Ft. Hall
FT. HALL RES.
(SHOSHONE)

WIND RIVER R.A.

Snake R.

WYOMING

Original land
of the
Plains Indians

Blackfeet

Plains
Cree

Blood
(CANADA)

Piegan

Assiniboine

Gross
Ventre

Mandan

MOUNTAIN AND
WESTERN INDIANS

PLAINS INDIANS

Crow

Santee
Sioux

COLORADO

Shoshoni

Teton
Sioux

Cheyenne

Yankton
Sioux

EASTERN

Paiute

Pawnee

Ponca

Iowa

Arapaho

Omaha

WOODLAND

Leadville

Kansa

Cheyenne

Osage

INDIANS

Kiowa
Apache

Comanche

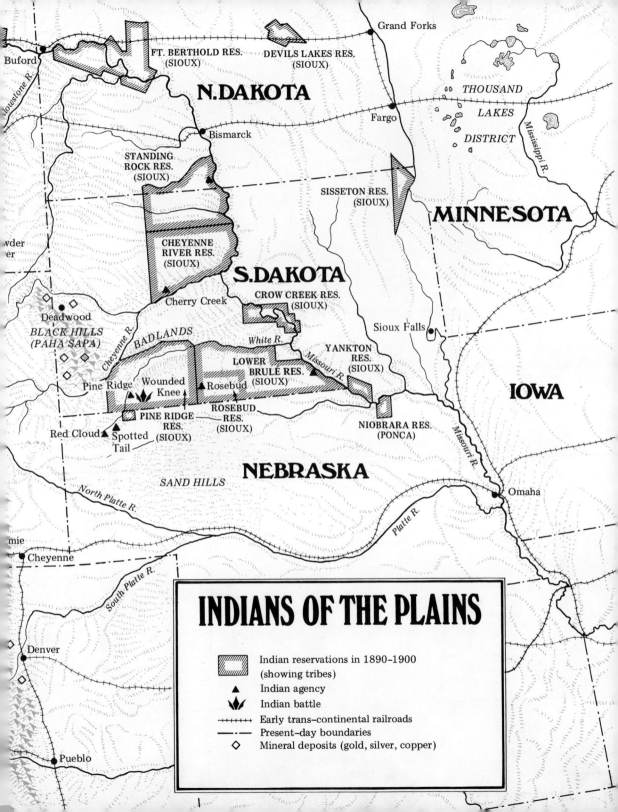

Grand Forks

Buford

Yellowstone R.

FT. BERTHOLD RES.
(SIOUX)

DEVILS LAKES RES.
(SIOUX)

THOUSAND

LAKES

Mississippi R.

N. DAKOTA

DISTRICT

Fargo

Bismarck

STANDING
ROCK RES.
(SIOUX)

SISSETON RES.
(SIOUX)

MINNESOTA

wder
er

CHEYENNE
RIVER RES.
(SIOUX)

S. DAKOTA

CROW CREEK RES.
(SIOUX)

Cherry Creek

Deadwood

*BLACK HILLS
(PAHA SAPA)*

Cheyenne R.

BADLANDS

White R.

Sioux Falls

LOWER
BRULE RES.
(SIOUX)

Missouri R.

YANKTON
RES.
(SIOUX)

IOWA

Pine Ridge

Wounded
Knee

Rosebud

Red Cloud

Spotted
Tail

PINE RIDGE
RES.
(SIOUX)

ROSEBUD
RES.
(SIOUX)

NIOBRARA RES.
(PONCA)

SAND HILLS

NEBRASKA

Missouri R.

Omaha

North Platte R.

Platte R.

mie
Cheyenne

South Platte R.

INDIANS OF THE PLAINS

Indian reservations in 1890–1900
(showing tribes)

▲ Indian agency

Indian battle

Early trans-continental railroads

Present-day boundaries

◇ Mineral deposits (gold, silver, copper)

Denver

Pueblo

FRANKLIN WATTS / NEW YORK / LONDON / 1976

INDIANS

OF

THE

PLAINS

SALLY SHEPPARD

A FIRST BOOK

FOR MY VERY GOOD FRIEND
FIGHTING BEAR, HUNKPAPA SIOUX

Photographs courtesy of:
American Museum of Natural History: p. 16; Library of Congress: p. 60, 63; Museum of the American Indian, Heye Foundation: pp. 9, 46, 64; National Collection of Fine Arts, Smithsonian Institution: p. 29; New York Public Library: p. 50; Smithsonian Institution, National Anthropological Archives: pp. 4, 12, 46, 69; Smithsonian Institution, National Anthropological Archives, Bureau of American Ethnology Collection: pp. 24, 32, 74; Smithsonian Office of Anthropology, Bureau of American Ethnology Collection: pp. 19, 20, 50; Union Pacific Railroad Museum: p. 54; United Press International: p. 83; U.S. Signal Corps: p. 35.

Cover design by Paul Gamarello

Library of Congress Cataloging in Publication Data

Sheppard, Sally.
    Indians of the Plains.

    (A First book)
    Bibliography: p.
    Includes index.
    SUMMARY: Describes the history, daily life, people, and culture of the various Indian tribes living on the Plains and discusses their present day life on the reservation.
    1. Indians of North America — Great Plains — Juvenile literature. [1. Indians of North America—Great Plains] I. Title.
E78.G73S45   979′.004′97   75–42219
ISBN 0–531–00847–9

CONTENTS

The People
1

Nation, Tribe, Band, Clan, and Family
3

Clothing
15

The Tepee
18

The Horse
23

The Buffalo
26

Religion
31

Myths and Legends
40

Music and Art
44

Leisure Activities
49

Wars and Heroes
52

How the West Was Lost
58

Counting Coup
66

Signs of the Times
68

Indian Orators
73

Reservation Life Today
78

For Further Reading
85

Index
86

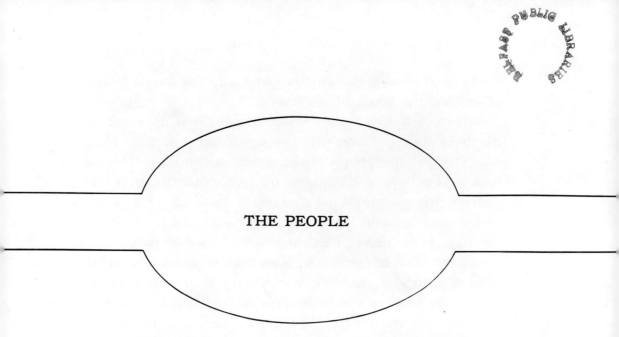

THE PEOPLE

The Plains have not always been grassy. Many thousands of years before the pioneers moved west, that great territory of the Dakotas, Nebraska, Montana, and Wyoming was largely dense hardwood forests. While there is archaeological evidence that man lived in these forests, we know very little about these early forest dwellers. Possibly they were nomadic groups. Most probably they lived on roots, berries, herbs, fowl, or small forest animals.

When the forest existed, the climate was warm and temperate. There were even palm trees and alligators as far north as the Dakotas. Then as the mountains to the west rose (a very gradual process that took thousands of years), the climate became more diversified and extreme. The emergence of the Rocky Mountains gradually cut off the moisture-bearing winds from the Pacific Ocean. This resulted in low summer rainfall and much drier winters. Gradually the forests disappeared and the grassy plains emerged.

No one knows exactly when humans first appeared in North America, but most scientists agree that they came from Asia. It is thought that the Bering Strait was once land linking Asia and North America. It is even possible that the strait was a fertile, grassy plain. What also seems apparent is that early prehistoric migrations were motivated by a quest for food. As the great herds moved eastward, small bands of people followed. But these migrations were not accomplished in a period of a few months or years. They took many thousands of years. Eventually, some of these Asian peoples reached what is now the northwestern corner of the United States. Some ultimately traveled farther south, and some were able to make their way across what is now western Canada, even to the Great Lakes area. The Plains Indians whom the white man encountered were the descendants of some of these peoples.

There were many, many different tribes of Indians on the Northern Plains, each with its own customs, life-style, and religious beliefs. It would be impossible to tell the story of each tribe in one book, so we will confine ourselves to the Sioux, the Cheyenne, the Crow, and the Blackfeet. Some of the other tribes who also frequented the Northern Plains before Indians were forced by the white man to lived in limited areas were the Kiowa, Ponca, Southern Cheyenne, Pawnee, Arapaho, Comanche, and Nez Percé.

NATION, TRIBE, BAND, CLAN, AND FAMILY

The largest unit of an Indian people was the nation or confederacy. This was a banding together of peoples with a common language root who were allies in peace and in war.

Next came the tribe, which in the case of the Cheyenne, Sioux, and Blackfeet was divided into bands. Bands were groups who joined together in a common cause such as hunting expeditions, warfare, or protection. Among the Crow, tribes were divided into clans. These groupings depended upon family or blood relationships, and one's clan membership was always the same as the mother's, not the father's.

Among some of the Plains Indians, tribal organizations and authority were very complicated. Authority rested with elected chiefs of the tribes, family, clan and/or band. No chieftainship was ever hereditary. Within a single family, the father or grandfather represented authority. Women were responsi-

SIOUX WARRIOR. THE ORIGINAL
WATERCOLOR BY KARL BODMER
WAS PAINTED AT FORT LOOKOUT,
A SIOUX AGENCY, IN 1833.

ble for small children and girls. As a boy reached adolescence, he came more and more under the influence of the male elders of his tribe.

The Sioux Nation

It is believed that the Indians who probably formed the Sioux Nation at the time the white man discovered America were living in the Thousand Lakes region of Minnesota. There they were known as the Oceti Sakowin, or SEVEN COUNCIL FIRES, because each council fire represented a different tribe. The tribes included the MDEWAKANTON, or Mystery Lake People, the WAHPETON, or Leaf People, the WAHPEKUTE, or Leaf Shooters, and the SISSETON, or Fish Scale People. (These four tribes were together known as the Santee and spoke the Dakota dialect of the Sioux language.) The three other council fires were the YANKTON and the YANKTONAI, who spoke the Nakota dialect, and the TETON. The Teton were the largest division of Sioux and were made up of seven bands who spoke the Lakota dialect: Oglala, Brulé, Miniconjou, Two Kettle, Sans Arc, Hunkpapa, and Sihasapa.

Usually the entire Sioux Nation, all seven council fires, met in council every year. At this gathering, people and leaders decided the nation's policy and endorsed or rejected future plans. There were forty-four elected chiefs in the council. Among these forty-four, four men served as a higher authority and had the power to elect one Supreme Chief. The four higher chiefs passed on plans proposed by their subordinates and acted on offenses against national unity and security. However, since the four higher chiefs met only once a year, actual power and authority was vested in individual tribal leaders or chiefs.

Although chieftainships were not inherited, an outstanding son of a chief was often elected to succeed his father or grandfather. To become a leader, a young man had to show bravery and fortitude, generosity and wisdom. He had to be able to provide for his tribe as a capable hunter, to protect his people as a brave warrior, and to show compassion and wisdom when dealing with offenses within his tribe.

The Cheyenne

Today's Cheyenne are the descendants of two related tribes — the TSĬS TSĬS TĂS, or Cheyenne proper, and the SUH TAI, who joined them sometime after the Tsĭs tsĭś tăs moved west across the Missouri River. It was originally believed that the name Cheyenne came from the French word *chien*, meaning "dog" — probably because an important warrior society of the tribe was called "Dog Soldiers." However, we now know that the name is an abbreviation of the Sioux term *Shā hī'yē na* or *Shā hī'ē la*, meaning "red talkers" or "people of alien speech."

The early origins of the Cheyenne are obscure. It is generally thought that they came from the northeast or east. According to Northern Cheyenne legend, the people lived for a long time on the border of a great water (possibly Lake Superior), the winter home of migrating waterfowl. From the great water they began their journey west. Cheyenne storytellers tell of their people moving by boat. They had few weapons and were unable to capture large animals except by occasional snaring. They ate such foods as skunks, waterfowl, and birds' eggs. The migration westward was filled with hardship, but eventually they made their way across the lakes and the Missouri River to the plains near the Black Hills of South Dakota.

Government and authority among the Cheyenne was not as formal as among the Sioux. Each band had its own leader or chief. But these leaders were advisers and did not give orders. For important decisions, councils of leaders met, and decisions were based on unanimous agreement. The Cheyenne did, however, have a complicated system of laws. Murder, for instance, was regarded as harmful to the whole tribe and was dealt with very sternly. Murderers were normally banished from the band. This usually meant death, because survival alone on the prairie wilderness was rare.

George Catlin, a painter who traveled and lived among the Indians during the middle 1800s and painted many hundreds of Indian portraits, described the Cheyenne in his journals:

> There is no finer race of men than these in North America, and none superior in stature, excepting the Osage, there being scarcely a man in the tribe full grown who is less than six feet in height. They are undoubtedly the richest in horses of any tribe on the continent. Living in the country as they do where great herds of wild horses are grazing on the prairies, which they catch in great numbers . . .

The Cheyenne were also known for their warrior societies, which were the foundation of tribal government. Every ten years the tribe met to choose forty chiefs. These forty, elected by members of the warrior societies, would then choose four Past Chiefs, or Old Men Chiefs, to serve as Supreme Advisers. There were no hereditary chiefs among the Cheyenne. Each warrior society had a Leading War Chief and nine Little War Chiefs. In total there were seventy-four chiefs, counting tribal rulers and warrior society chiefs. These included four Old Men Chiefs, forty Tribal Big Chiefs, three Leading War Chiefs, and twenty-seven Little War Chiefs. All told, there were six warrior societies, or soldier bands, of the Cheyenne. They included: Kit Fox, Elk Soldiers, Dog Men, Red Shields, Crazy Dogs, and Bow Strings. A seventh band called Chief Soldiers was made up of the forty-four tribal chieftains. Almost all young, able-bodied, and ambitious men of the tribe belonged to one of the warrior societies. However, membership was not mandatory. These warrior societies were in fact an organized military force that also acted as a camp police force.

Membership in the warrior societies was not hereditary, although most young boys joined their father's or grandfather's band. A boy joined from the age of thirteen to sixteen. His mother and father accompanied him to the first society dance, and a gift of two or three horses was often given. He might give his gift to the chief of the society, to a dancer, or to a poor woman, but a gift was obligatory. The candidate was received into the society without any special ceremony.

Each soldier band had four young women members, usually unmarried. They were present at meetings, participated in singing and dancing, and sometimes cooked for the soldiers. These girls were called *Nŭt ūhk e å*, or "female soldier." If a woman member married, she resigned her position and a replacement was chosen.

A GROUP OF CHEYENNE MEN PREPARING FOR
MEDICINE LODGE CEREMONIES IN
THE EARLY PART OF THE TWENTIETH CENTURY

The Crow

The Crow Indians were originally part of a large group of Indians in the upper Missouri River region. According to legend a dispute between two chiefs resulted in a division. One group remained, while those we know as Crow Indians moved westward. Often the Crow refer to themselves as ABSÁROKÂ, meaning "Bird People." The name Crow comes from a translation of the French *gens des corbeaux*, which is French for "people of the crow."

In the middle of the 1830s George Catlin, who painted portraits of many Crow Indians, described them, saying:

> There is a sort of ease and grace added to their dignity of manners which gives them the air of gentlemen at once. I observed the other day that most of them were over six feet high and very many of these have cultivated their natural hair to such an almost incredible length that it sweeps the ground as they walk. . . . They usually oil their hair with a profusion of bear's grease every morning . . . and this extraordinary length of hair among the Crows is confined to the men alone.

There were two divisions among the Crow Indians — RIVER CROW and MOUNTAIN CROW. The River Crow were named because they left the mountain section about 1859 and lived along the Missouri River. The Mountain Crow were so named because of their custom of hunting and roaming near the mountains away from the Missouri River.

The Crow were divided into thirteen clans, each clan having a distinctive name such as Burned Mouth, Newly Made

Lodges, Whistling Waters, Big Lodges, and Kicked in the Bellies. The thirteen clans were linked together into six loose groups often called PHRATRIES. Membership in a clan was inherited through the mother's side only, the Crow being a matriarchal society. In other words, a child's clan affiliation was to the people of his mother, rather than to those of his father.

Among the Crow, cousins of the same generation are brothers and sisters. For example, an uncle or aunt's child (whom you would call a first cousin) a Crow child would call a brother or sister. Crow men call any man directly related by blood "brother" regardless of generation. However, the women call each other "sister" only if they are of the same generation.

Each clan had a headman who became the chief by virtue of his success as a warrior and hunter. There was no one central chief who commanded supreme power. However, at important events such as a buffalo hunt or a battle, those chiefs who had been particularly brave were looked to for leadership. One of these chiefs acted as camp chief, selecting the campsite. He was elected by the council of chiefs who ruled over the united tribe when it met. Only chiefs were entitled to debate matters of tribal interest. One of the military societies was appointed by the camp chief every spring to serve as police, but the actions of the police could be vetoed by the chief.

According to Plenty Coups, a Crow chief who lived between 1850 and 1932 and told his biography to a white writer, Frank B. Linderman:

A man or woman was born to a clan. Within the Crow Nation there were many secret societies such as the Foxes, the Warclubs, the Big Dogs, Crazy Dogs, Muddy

PLENTY COUPS, A CROW.
THIS 1880 PHOTOGRAPH SHOWS
THE TYPICAL CROW HAIRDRESS
AND THE FRINGED BUCKSKIN SHIRT
AND ELABORATE BEADED TRIMMINGS
WORN BY THE PLAINS INDIANS.

Hands and others. Membership in the secret societies was an honor which most young men aspired to. Societies elected their members upon petition. Any warrior who had "counted coups" was eligible.

Blackfoot Confederacy

The Blackfoot Confederacy was made up of three tribes — the SIKSIKA, or Blackfeet Proper; the PIEGAN; and the KAINAH, or Bloods. It is generally believed that the Blackfeet were so named because their moccasins were constantly discolored by the ashes of prairie fires. It is also thought by some that the name referred to the habit of wearing black-dyed moccasins. The Bloods were perhaps named because of their red-earth sacred face paint. The name Piegan meant "Poor Robes." The Blackfeet originally lived north of the Canadian border and held an immense territory stretching almost from the North Saskatchewan River in Canada to the southern headwaters of the Missouri River in Montana.

Although one refers to the "Blackfoot Confederacy," the tribes were not politically united under a single government. However, the three divisions spoke the same language and regarded themselves as one people. Because their cultures were so alike, they have always been regarded as a single tribe.

Each of the three tribes was composed of bands held together by blood relationships and friendship. The Piegan, the largest tribe, had twenty-three bands; the Bloods and Blackfeet each had six. Each band had chiefs, but a chieftainship was not a formal office. Chiefs were the outstanding persons among any number of men chosen as headmen. Band chieftains rarely made individual decisions, but rather acted upon the advice of headmen.

During tribal assemblies, headmen from the bands usually designated one man as chief and spokesman. The function of a headman was as guardian and defendant of the social order. But above all, he was to preserve tribal peace. A person with a grievance against another member of his band could appeal to the headmen, and the headmen were expected to solve the problem without violence. Although each tribe had chiefs, the head chief of the confederacy was chosen by mutual agreement. His main function was to call council meetings, and he could influence the decision as to who would be invited. Every matter of importance was decided by council. Councils usually met in the summer. After the fall hunting season, bands went their separate ways and regathered in the springtime. The only time at which the whole tribal government functioned was at the time of the Sun Dance.

Like many other Plains Indians, the Blackfeet had warrior societies that exercised much influence at council meetings. The most important was the All Comrades.

CLOTHING

The typical clothing of the Plains Indian man was a shirt, breechclout, and leggings of tan buckskin. The leggings were fastened to a waist strap and were sometimes fringed and decorated with porcupine quills and, later on, with beadwork. These long leggings were actually the origin of the Western cowboy's leather chaps.

During the winter months the Indians would stuff their leather-soled moccasins with grass or hair for warmth. This, together with the long leggings and a buffalo robe worn hair side in, would keep a man warm in the often subzero weather of the Plains. On occasion a loose jacket made of deer or elk skins was worn. Sometimes it was in the form of a poncho without sleeves.

The women generally wore a long shirtdress with wide cape sleeves, a belt, leggings to the knees, and moccasins.

THIS BLACKFOOT MOUNTAIN CHIEF
WEARS A FULL FEATHERED HEADDRESS,
SYMBOL OF MANY BRAVE EXPLOITS.

The men usually wore their hair long, often braided. In some instances it was possible to recognize an Indian's tribal connection simply by his hairdo. The Crow, for example, dressed their hair with bear grease and brushed it back from the forehead into a pompadour.

Headdresses varied from tribe to tribe. Feathers were symbols of achievement and worn usually only on special occasions such as ceremonial dances, councils, or the warpath. Only the Plains Indians wore true warbonnets made of eagle feathers. Each eagle feather of a man's headdress represented an exploit, and each feather was marked to designate a particular act of bravery. An eagle-feather warbonnet was highly valued, and one perfect tail of twelve feathers, white with black tips, was worth one pony. Most Plains warriors wore only golden eagle feathers.

THE TEPEE

Life on the Plains was a continual battle against the elements. Summers were often hot, dry, and windy. Winter temperatures could fall as low as thirty degrees below zero, and snowdrifts might reach ten to twelve feet. Getting enough to eat was a constant worry to the Plains Indians. Since food was not always close at hand, the Plains people often had to travel miles before finding the necessary game or fowl. And since the hunters were often on the move, it was important that their housing be easily moved. The tepee was perfect. (The tepee should not be confused with the wigwam. The tepee was pointed at the top and looked rather like a funnel set on its broad base. The wigwam, on the other hand, was a rounded arched framework in the shape of a beehive, often overlaid with bark, which in turn was covered with hides. The tepee also had an opening at the top through which smoke from the fire could escape.

A VILLAGE NEAR THE MOUTH OF
THE YELLOWSTONE RIVER, IN 1878.
WOMEN ARE DRESSING BUFFALO HIDES,
WHILE BUFFALO MEAT IS DRYING
IN THE SUN ON THE RACKS
IN FRONT OF THE TEPEES.

A BLACKFOOT WOMAN MOUNTED ON
A HORSE PULLING A TRAVOIS

The word *wigwam* is an Algonquian word. *Tepee* is from the Siouan word meaning "they dwell.")

The tepee was made of long poles, arranged in a circle and brought together near the top. The poles were often twenty-five feet high. They were covered with from fifteen to eighteen buffalo skins that had been sewn together to form a single piece. The skins were secured by means of wooden pins and ground pegs. The diameter of the tepee was about fifteen feet. The door to the tepee consisted of a flap of skin stretched over a frame. In the center of the tepee was a fire pit for warmth and cooking. The smoke escaped through the opening at the top of the tepee, where the supporting poles crossed. There were three beds, or seats — one at each side and one at the back. The beds were long platforms covered with mats of light willow rods over which were thrown buffalo robes or blankets. Sometimes the outside of the tepees were decorated with pictographs illustrating Indian life, particularly hunting and war exploits.

The setting up, care, packing, and moving of the tepee were the responsibility of the woman of the family. She tanned the hides, sewed them together, and put up the tepee. Several women, working together, could set up a tepee in three minutes' time. They could just as easily take it down.

Before the horse, tepees were somewhat smaller and were transported by dog travois. Later, the horse made it possible to move larger tepees. The travois was a sort of sledge or litter. The tepee poles were tied into two equal bunches by rawhide ropes strung through holes at the end of the poles. The two bunches of poles were then bound on each side of the horse so that the upper ends of the poles rested about the animal's shoulders while the lower ends dragged on the ground behind. The tepee cover was made into a compact bundle and tied over the poles behind the horse. Other household equipment could also be piled on top of the tepee covering, and sometimes old people and children traveled this way.

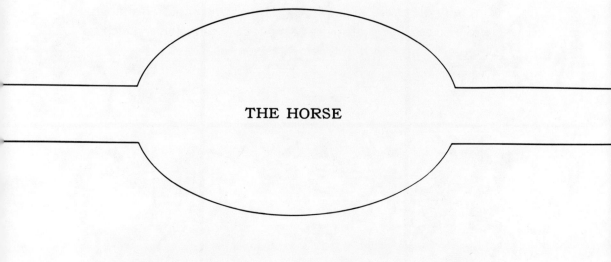

THE HORSE

One single event probably more than anything else changed the life and economy of the Plains Indian — the introduction of the horse. The Spanish brought the horse to the Southwest during the sixteenth century. Although they tried to keep the native peoples from learning to ride and manage them, some horses were inevitably stolen. By the middle of the seventeenth century, Apaches and Ute were systematically raiding Spanish settlements in the Southwest for horses. When the Pueblo Indians of New Mexico rose against the Spaniards, large herds of horses were acquired.

In the first half of the eighteenth century, the horse was introduced into the Northern Plains by the Shoshoni. The Shoshoni migrated north from Utah, Nevada, and Texas after severing their ties with the Comanche on the Southern Plains. About 1730 the Shoshoni warriors on horseback attacked and

THIS PICTORIAL AUTOBIOGRAPHY DRAWN
BY RUNNING ANTELOPE, A HUNKPAPA SIOUX,
IN 1873 ILLUSTRATES THE
IMPORTANCE OF THE HORSE
IN PLAINS INDIAN LIFE.

easily defeated the foot soldiers of their traditional rivals, the Blackfeet. After this humiliating defeat the Blackfeet sought help from friendly Cree and Assiniboine, who gave them another secret weapon — ten guns that could kill a man at a distance. The next time the Blackfeet confronted the Shoshoni, both groups were on foot but the Blackfeet had the guns and soon sent the Shoshoni fleeing. It was not long before Blackfeet tribes had enough guns and horses to dominate much of the Northern Plains territory.

Soon all the Indians of the Plains acquired horses, either by trading or by stealing. Raiding other camps and stealing horses was considered a sport, as well as a necessity. With the horse it was possible to travel many more miles per day than on foot. The horse also facilitated surprise attacks, because escape could be made at great speed.

The horse also became a status symbol and a primary bartering item. Horses were given by a bridegroom's family to the parents of the bride and one's wealth was often measured by the number of horses one owned. It was considered a prime virtue to give horses away to the needy. Ultimately the Indians became so adept at horsemanship that one famous Indian fighter, General Philip Sheridan, called them "the greatest light cavalry in the world."

THE BUFFALO

It is difficult to imagine the vast herds of buffalo that roamed the open spaces from the Mexican border north into Canada. There were millions of these shaggy-coated, magnificent beasts when the white man first began to explore the West. Sometimes one herd blackened the horizon for as far as the human eye could see.

It was the buffalo that made life possible on the grassy and often arid northwestern Plains. The buffalo supplied the Indians not only with food but with clothing and shelter. Their meat provided food. Their hides were used for warm clothing, robes, and tepees. The sinew was made into bowstrings and sewing equipment. Bones were fashioned for cooking utensils and even children's toys. The rawhide made fine lacings and moccasin soles. Another important use of buffalo rawhide was to make parfleches. These were skin boxes or pouches used to carry small utensils, personal effects, and dried meat. They ranged from large rectangular boxes to small envelope-shaped pouches. Warbonnets were often carried in special cylinder-shaped parfleches. The parfleches for carrying ceremonial or religious objects were often elaborately decorated with quills or beadwork.

Before the horse, buffalo were hunted on foot and with bow and arrow. Sometimes a hunter would wear the skin of a wolf or buffalo to cover up his human scent. This way, he could get very close to the buffalo and let fly with an arrow at close range.

In the summer large buffalo hunts were organized by a whole band or tribe. When scouts reported a herd of buffalo near, the people would line up in two columns, making a corridor between them. They would then stamp and wave robes or blankets to make the buffalo run at full speed down the corridor, which inevitably led to the edge of a steep cliff. Since the buffalo were running at a full gallop, it was impossible for the lead buffalo to stop before it went over the edge of the cliff. So over it went, followed by the rest of the herd. Usually, most of the buffalo were killed. The wounded ones were finished off by Indian hunters waiting at the bottom of the cliff. Alternatively, the buffalo were driven into a corral and then shot with arrows or clubbed to death.

Once the horse was introduced to the Plains Indians, the buffalo hunt took on a new look and became a test of the hunter's skill as a rider and marksman. Hunting the buffalo took considerable skill, for they are formidable beasts and when stampeded can easily trample to death both men and horses. A buffalo bull may weigh as much as two thousand pounds.

George Catlin described the Indian method of hunting buffalo with bow and arrow from horseback:

In the chase of the buffalo or other animal, the Indian generally "strips" himself and his horse by throwing off his shield and quiver and every part of his dress which might be an encumbrance to him in running, grasping his bow in his left hand, with five or six arrows drawn from his quiver, and ready for instant use. In his right hand (or attached to the wrist) is a heavy whip which he uses without mercy and forces his horse alongside his game at the swiftest speed. . . .

When pursuing a large herd, the Indian generally rides close in the rear until he selects the animal he wishes to kill, which he separates from the throng as soon as he can by placing his horse between it and the herd and forcing it off by itself where he can approach it without the danger of being trampled to death to which he is often liable by too closely escorting the multitude. . . . Then with the halter lying loose on the horse's neck, the rider leant forward and off from the side of his horse. At the instant he was opposite the buffalo's body, he let go with his arrow.

As soon as the arrow left the bow, the Indian hunter would veer his horse away from the wounded and angry animal to avoid being gored. Sometimes, instead of a bow and arrow being used, a lance was thrust into the side of a buffalo while rider and horse ran at full speed and then veered off sharply.

In the old days, Plains Indian hunters were careful not to

BUFFALO CHASE—COW AND CALF,
PAINTED BY GEORGE CATLIN IN THE 1830s

be wasteful. They believed that indiscriminate killing would cause the buffalo to leave and thus bring starvation to the tribe. However, the Indian changed when the white man came and killed great numbers of buffalo to clear the land for grazing cattle and sheep and to collect the large pieces for buffalo skins. According to George Bird Grinnell, a noted observer of the American Indian during the last half of the nineteenth and early part of the twentieth century:

> ... after the Winchester repeater came into use, it seemed as if the different tribes vied with each other in wanton slaughter. Provided with one of these weapons and a couple of belts of cartridges, the hunters would run as long as their horses could keep up with the band and literally cover the prairie with carcasses, many of which were never skinned.

The slaughter of thousands upon thousands of buffalo by both white and Indian hunters brought not only economic hardship to the Plains Indians, but even death from starvation. In fact, both white men and Indians share in the blame for the disappearance of the great buffalo herds, but perhaps the blame falls more heavily on the white man because it was he who brought the Winchester repeater to the Indian.

RELIGION

The Indians believed in one Supreme Being. They also believed that since the Great Spirit had created the universe and all the creatures in it, he had endowed *all living objects* with a soul.

All tribes had various ritual dances during which they asked help from the Great Spirit. Often before a buffalo hunt they would apologize to the Great Unseen Buffalo, or supernatural leader of the animal, for having to kill the buffalo. Indians believed, as many whites do, that good acts are rewarded and evil ones punished. Among the Plains Indians the vow to perform a ceremony or other act agreeable to the "powers" was considered a means of gaining their goodwill or of atoning for past offenses.

A GROUP OF MEN SEATED IN A SWEAT LODGE
WITH THE COVERING PARTLY RAISED,
SHOWING THE FRAMEWORK. TAKEN ON THE
ROSEBUD RESERVATION, SOUTH DAKOTA, IN 1898.

Sweat Lodge Ceremony

It was customary for a young man at the beginning of his manhood to undergo the Sweat Lodge Ceremony. This ceremony was also used by warriors before a battle, by hunters before a big hunt, and before periods of fasting. The frame for the sweat lodge was made of willow rods bent to form a hemispherical shape. It was covered with skins and was large enough to accommodate several people. A hole was dug near the door into which heated stones were put. These were sprinkled with water to generate steam. The doorway was then covered with a flap of skin.

The purpose of the sweat bath, not unlike the modern-day sauna, was a means of purifying the body. In the sweat lodge many prayers were offered. At the conclusion the participants would plunge themselves into a stream. After the Sweat Lodge Ceremony the young man was taken by some of the men (usually including his father and uncles) to a remote spot and was left, wearing only moccasins and a breechclout. He spent the next three days praying and without food or water, exposed to the burning sun, rain, and cold prairie nights. This was done to strip him of all superficiality or things of the flesh. During this time it was expected that he would have a meaningful dream or vision. At the end of the third or fourth day, he was brought down in a considerably weakened state.

Upon his return to camp he was given a few drops of water at a time and some food. After he was bathed and fed, his advisers and the holy man of the tribe would attempt to interpret his dream. The vision or dream was believed to be a direct communication between man and the supernatural. The young man might dream of a human spirit, such as a long-dead grandfather, or of an animal or bird, or even an inanimate object. Often his adult name came directly from his vision, and he might take the spirit of his vision as his personal charm. For example, if he dreamed of the hawk, he would believe that the spirit of the hawk would protect him, and he might wear its feathers as assurance against misfortune. If he dreamed of the bear, he would probably wear bearskin or carry a piece of bearskin, a bear tooth, or some such relic as protection against the forces of evil.

Among many Plains Indians, dreaming of a phenomenon or a bird or animal was believed to give the dreamer special powers over the object of the dream. Those who dreamed of thunder and lightning by tradition became clowns and were supposed to have special powers to protect others and themselves from lightning. These contrary men or *heyoka,* as the Sioux called them, did such things as walking upside down, wearing a face mask on the back of their head, and wearing little clothing in cold weather and too much in hot. In other words, their actions had to be contrary to the norm. They also acted as clowns to lift the hearts of their people in times of sorrow.

Sun Dance

The Plains Indians, like Indians in other parts of the country, were deeply religious people. There were many ceremonial dances, but the one common to almost all Plains Indians was the Sun Dance. Although some details differed from tribe to

DURING THE SUN DANCE CEREMONIES,
FRIENDS AND RELATIVES SANG AND
PRAISED THE DANCERS FOR THEIR COURAGE.

tribe, the general meaning of the Sun Dance was universal among Plains Indians.

Probably the best known is the Sioux Sun Dance, which is still performed on Sioux reservations in North and South Dakota. Among the Sioux the Sun Dance was an annual event held each year during the moon of the ripening chokecherries. The men who danced had made vows to perform the ceremony in return for one of four favors granted by the Supreme Powers: a life spared in battle, the recovery of a sick child, the end of a famine or epidemic, and finally, an abundance of food and prosperity for the tribe.

All told, the preparations for the ceremony lasted twelve days. The first four days were a time of conviviality during which the shamans (religious leaders) chose individuals to be assistants to the dance. These assistants served as a symbolic hunter, digger, escort, or singer. To be chosen was a great honor. Young women relatives of the dancers were named as attendants.

The second four-day period was spent in secret preparation and instruction for those who had made special vows to dance. Often one shaman, called a mentor, was responsible for the overall supervision and instructions. He was also responsible for the administration of the whole Sun Dance camp.

The last four days might be called the Holy Days. During this time a large circular arbor of poles covered with leafy branches was erected in the center of the camp. To the east the sacred lodge, where the dancers received final instructions, was built. While the sacred lodge was under construction, the hunter scouted for the cottonwood tree that would serve as the sacred pole.

When the tree was selected, the hunter notified the mentor. A Buffalo Dance was held, during which time the Sun Dance was blessed. Then the tree was chopped down and brought to its ceremonial place. The tree itself symbolized the enemy. Chopping it down and bringing it into camp was symbolic of capturing and killing an enemy. When the pole was brought to the center of the dance lodge, it was painted so that the side facing west would be red; north, blue; east, green; and south, yellow.

The pole was raised and placed in the hole with great care, for the Sioux believed that if it fell to the ground they would suffer the worst kind of bad luck, perhaps even famine or decisive defeat in battle. From the crosspiece of the pole were hung two effigies made from rawhide — a buffalo and a man. The buffalo effigy was in fact an offering to Wakan Tanka, the Sioux Great Spirit, for a plentiful supply of buffalo meat during the coming year. The man effigy symbolized victory over their enemies in time of war.

Before dawn of the fourth day the mentor and shamans went to a nearby hill to greet the rising sun and pray for a fine day. They asked Sky to give strength to the dancers and Bear to give wisdom to the mentor and shamans. According to Luther Standing Bear, a Brulé Sioux who lived from the 1860s to 1939:

From each tipi came six, eight and sometimes ten from a band to dance. There was a leader who carried a pipe of peace; the others followed one by one. They wore buffalo robes with the hair outside, and quite resembled a band of buffalo coming to a stream to drink. . . .

The medicine man came forward and took charge of four or eight of the dancers. Four of them must be painted alike. They put on beautiful headdresses richly ornamented with porcupine quills. Their wrists were wound around with sagebrush, and the eagle-bone whistles they used were likewise decorated.

This was a very solemn affair. These men were to dance for three or four days without food or water. Some of their relatives cried; others sang to praise them and make them feel courageous. . . .

The braves started dancing as soon as the sun started to rise. They stood facing the sun with both hands raised above their heads, the eagle-bone whistles in their mouths, and they blew on these every time the singers hit the skin with their sticks. All day long they stood in one position, facing the sun, until it set.

The dance was kept up until one of the participants fainted, when he was laid out on a bed of sagebrush. Luther Standing Bear describes the painful and sacrificial part of the dance which occurred on the next day: "First he [a dancer] would walk all around the hall so that all could see him. Then he went straight to the pole. He was giving himself for a living sacrifice." This means he would undergo the agony of being suspended from the pole by his own flesh.

There were two groups of dancers — those who were suspended from the pole and those who vowed to "gaze at the sun continuously." The ceremony was opened to slow, measured music. As the dance continued, the tempo of the music increased. There were several intermissions, during which time the dancers could rest. During the dance, friends and relatives of the dancers would sing and praise him for his courage.

According to Luther Standing Bear: "After the dance was over, everybody moved away, going where he pleased. It was a free country then. But afterward, if we ever returned to that sacred spot where the pole was yet standing, with the crosspiece attached, we stood for a long time in reverent attitude, because it was a sacred place to us."

MYTHS AND LEGENDS

All Indian peoples have many legends ranging from their own version of the story of creation to how the turtle got its hard shell. One interesting story is related by Two Leggings, a Crow warrior:

> We have always believed in one creator of everything and call him First Worker. One day First Worker was looking over the world and did not like all this water. He made a duck dive down and bring him some mud. After rubbing this between his palms he blew it everywhere, creating the land and mountains and rivers. First Worker wanted to make human beings and formed the mud into many groups of clay people. To test them he made arrows and stuck them into the ground pointing east. When he ordered the first group of clay people to charge the arrows, they fell back. The next group also stopped when

they met the arrows. Although the last group were pierced by the arrows, they ran on through. These different clay peoples became the different Indian tribes, and the bravest who had charged through became the Crows.

First Worker was proud of them because they were not afraid to die. He told the other groups to spread out and live in different places but he placed the Crows in the center so that whatever direction they traveled they would always meet other tribes.

First Worker also created two boys and ordered them to teach the Crows how to live and give them their religion. These boys were First Worker's servants and that is why when we dream and have visions we receive both a medicine and a sacred helper to guide us through life. Except for important ceremonial occasions and when we fast for visions, we address our prayers to our sacred helper, who will pray for us to the First Worker. These helpers are different for each of us as we all have different dreams.

One Sioux legend tells of a bear who wanted to climb up to a bright star and sit on it, looking over all the land far and wide. His mother said, "No, you had better climb a tall tree and look over the land from a treetop. You know how to hug a tree, but you do not know how to hoghold a star." However, the bear did not heed his mother's warning. So one day when a large cloud came that reached from the land up to the star, the bear walked up and over the cloud onto the star. There he sat on his haunches looking over all the land and among the stars. He liked this a lot. Suddenly the star became a shooting star. It raced through the air faster than the swiftest bird, and the

(41)

bear held on for dear life. The bear prayed to his mother, say-ing, "Mother, mother, help me." But his mother said, "Don't bawl and cry. Be brave. You shouldn't have hugged that star, you should have hugged a tree. But be brave." The bear was brave but full of fear as he went hurtling through the air, hug-ging the star as hard as he could. Finally, a large eagle soaring high saw the bear on the star. The bear had become so small and shrunken with fear that he was only the size of a rabbit. The eagle seized him with his talons and carried him away to a hilltop and ate him. Just then another very large and very strong eagle appeared. It was the bear. He had been so brave in mind and soul amid all the danger and fear that he had been changed into this large and strong eagle with broad-moving wings to carry him way up on high far above the clouds.

A Dakota Sioux legend aptly represents the philosophy of the Plains Indians. It tells of White Buffalo Woman, who offered a sacred pipe and small round stone and said:

> With this sacred pipe you will walk upon the Earth; for the Earth is your Grandmother and Mother, and She is sacred. Every step that is taken upon Her should be as a prayer. The bowl of this pipe is of red stone; it is the Earth. Carved in the stone and facing the center is this buffalo calf who represents all the four-leggeds who live upon your Mother. The stem of the pipe is of wood and this represents all that grows upon the earth. And those 12 feathers which hang here where the stem fits into the bowl are from Wanbli Galeshka, the Spotted Eagle, and they represent the eagle and all the winged of the air. All these peoples and all the things of the universe are

joined to you who smoke the pipe — all send their voices to Wakan Tanka, the Great Spirit. When you pray with this pipe, you pray for and with everything.

With this pipe you will be bound to all your relatives: Your Grandmother and Father, your Grandmother and Mother. This round rock, which is made of the same red stone as the bowl of the pipe, your Father Wakan Tanka has also given to you. It is the Earth, your Grandmother and Mother, and it is where you will live and increase. This Earth which He has given to you is red; and the Great Spirit has also given to you a red day, and a red road (the good straight road of purity and life). All of this is sacred and so do not forget! Every dawn as it comes is a holy event and every day is holy for the light comes from your Father Wakan Tanka, and also you must remember that the two-leggeds and all other peoples who stood upon the Earth are sacred and should be treated as such.

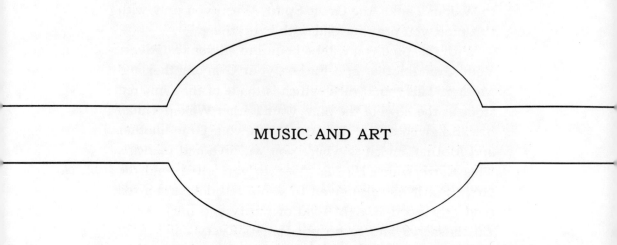

MUSIC AND ART

Everyday clothing and utensils were generally simple and functional. However, the Indians, with their reverence for nature, also had an eye for beauty. Men and women alike were artistic and skillful. They fashioned beautiful and elaborate ceremonial clothing, quillwork, drawings, and pipes. Even everyday objects such as babies' cradleboards were decorated.

Plains Indian women are famous throughout the world for their fine and elaborate beadwork. Before glass beads were introduced by white people to the Plains Indians, the women used porcupine quills dyed with natural vegetable dyes and earth pigments. Intricate patterns were included in the quillwork, many of them symbolic of various tribal beliefs and customs. By 1800 glass beads were being introduced to the Plains Indians, and within fifty years the beadwork of the Plains Indian women was highly developed. The technique of beadwork was devised solely by the Indian and was not a craft introduced by the whites.

Moccasins were often decorated with beads and still are. A pair of totally beaded moccasins today costs in the neighborhood of $250. Even handmade moccasins with a small amount of beadwork are expensive.

The tanning and curing of hides was also an art, and the work of the women of the tribe. The women also fashioned and decorated the elaborate ceremonial dresses of their men. However, not only the women were gifted as artists. Many men decorated the outside of their tepees with paintings and drawings of their war and hunting exploits.

One of the most famous of all Indian artists of the nineteenth century was Amos Bad Heart Bull, an Oglala Sioux and a member of a distinguished family of band historians. These men who painted the tribal history in pictures were as honored as hunters and warriors. One could identify individuals in the pictures, not because of any particular physical resemblance, but by such things as a shield, warbonnet, bead designs, and so on. Although the warrior probably may not have won these particular objects in a battle, they were added in the picture for identification.

After the Battle of the Little Bighorn, Amos Bad Heart Bull faithfully recorded the defeat of General George Custer in pictures on buffalo hides. The drawings are full of action and show the Indian custom of painting their horses in pastel colors. For a long time these famous paintings were not known to the world at large, but eventually the artist's family agreed to their publication. Today these drawings can be found in a book called *A Pictographic History of the Oglala Sioux.*

Pictorial records of the Custer battle were also depicted by Cheyenne artists. One example, that of High Bull, can be seen at the Museum of the American Indian in New York City. Another example of fine pictograph art is that of Red Crane, a Blackfoot warrior. His painting is on a skin that was once part of the lining of a lodge. It depicts the most important events of his life, such as shooting an elk, killing an enemy with bow and arrow, taking scalps, and meeting up with two charging grizzly bears. Such drawings were, in fact, the Indian way of keeping a diary.

Music

Music as well as dance was an important part of Plains Indian tribal life. For every public ceremony, as well as each important act in the career of an individual, there was a special song. Various ceremonies had their peculiar rhythms and songs that

ABOVE: BEADWORK, PIPES, WAR CLUBS, AND OTHER EXAMPLES OF SIOUX ARTISTIC SKILL IN DECORATING BOTH CEREMONIAL AND EVERYDAY OBJECTS. BELOW: THIS RECORD OF THE BATTLE OF THE LITTLE BIGHORN, SHOWING GENERAL CUSTER AT LEFT CENTER, WAS PAINTED ON DEERSKIN BY A CHEYENNE WHO FOUGHT IN THE BATTLE.

pertained to individual acts such as fasting and prayer, setting up tepees, hunting, courtship, playing games, and facing and defying death. An Indian can determine at once the class of a strange song by the rhythm of the music. Some songs are wordless, while others may have many verses of words. The men sing in a very high-pitched falsetto, and the women also use a high, reedy sound an octave above the men's.

Clans and societies had special officers who ensured the exact rendition of their songs. Members alone had the right to sing, and a penalty was exacted from the member who made a mistake in singing. Sometimes one could purchase a song from its owner. The women composed and sang the lullabies and spinning and grinding songs.

In ceremonial prayer songs accuracy was essential. Otherwise "the path would not be straight" and the prayers could not reach the proper destination. This could result in disaster. For this reason, when an error was made in singing, the singer stopped at once and began over again. Prompters kept strict watch during ceremonies to forestall accidents.

The musical instruments of the Plains Indians were drums of various shapes and sizes, flutes, bone whistles, and rattles sometimes made of turtle shells. The drum rhythms were often different from the rhythm of the songs. The drum might be beaten in 2/4 time and the song sung in 3/4 time. The dancers followed the rhythm of the drum, not the song. Today in many parts of the country one can attend Indian ceremonials and watch the dancers decked out in their traditional finery.

LEISURE ACTIVITIES

Even though life on the Plains was difficult, the Plains Indians were not without their moments of fun. Both children and adults engaged in games of amusement and skill. Young boys played many "learning" games, such as pretending to hunt buffalo or battle with other boys representing the enemy. Little girls also played "learning games" that centered around their future duties as adults.

In the winter the Cheyenne made sleds of buffalo ribs for sliding down hills. These sleds were used only by men and boys, but girls and young women made toboggans from a slab split from a tree. The buffalo-rib sled went faster than a horse could run.

In the summer both boys and girls spent much time in the water. Both sexes were expert swimmers. Spinning tops was a favorite game among boys. The tops were made of cot-

tonwood or ash, with a bone point or peg. The strings were made of twisted milkweed fibers. The contest was to see who could spin his top farthest on the hard ground or ice.

Wrestling or *Ni' hi wän üh* was a favorite sport of the Cheyenne, as it was of other tribes. Cheyenne boys began to wrestle at the age of seven or eight. They never used the feet or legs in tripping, but tried to swing the opponent off his feet or bend him back by brute strength. They were very wiry and strong, and it took considerable agility and strength to throw a man.

Another favorite game of Plains Indians was "hoop and pole," a Plains version of a game called *Chunkeyivas* played by Gulf Coast and southern tribes east of the Mississippi River. A large wooden hoop was interlaced with rawhide straps (much like the crisscross lacing of the snowshoe) to form a net. Most tribes rolled the hoop and tried to stop it by spearing it. Some Plains Indian tribesmen tossed the hoop in the air and tried to hit it with pronged sticks.

ABOVE: SIOUX WOMEN PLAY A GAME OF DICE.
BELOW: A GAME OF HOOP AND POLE PLAYED IN
A VILLAGE NEAR FORT CLARK, NORTH DAKOTA.

WARS AND HEROES

Old-time Hollywood movies to the contrary, Western Plains Indians were not uncivilized and did not make a practice of attacking white people for the sport of it.

The Indians had many grievances against the whites. Fur traders trapped indiscriminately to sell their pelts for high prices back East. Hunters needlessly slaughtered thousands of buffalo and other game. In addition, as settlers began to take over land and build homes, fences went up and trespassing by Indians very often resulted in dead Indians.

To understand the impact of these events, one must remember the Indian philosophy that the Great Spirit created the land for the use of all his creatures. As Tashunka Witko, or Crazy Horse, the famous Oglala Sioux chief and warrior, said, "One does not sell the earth upon which the people walk."

These conflicts, many born of different beliefs and customs, eventually led to the defeat and humiliation of the Indian people and to the death of many, both Indians and whites. Revenge for injustice was a basic tenet of Indian philosophy, although they were not above peaceful and negotiated settlement of disputes. When the pipe was smoked and Indians agreed, that agreement was binding and to break one's word was a disgraceful act. Although many honorable white men were involved in treaties with the Indians, others were greedy and dishonorable.

Land was only one of the riches sought by the whites. Gold and other mineral deposits inflamed the conflicts. In fact, it was the discovery of gold in the Black Hills of South Dakota that led to some of the bloodiest battles between Indian warriors and white soldiers.

In 1868 a treaty with the Indians stated, "No white person or persons shall be permitted to settle upon or occupy any portion of the territory without the consent of the Indians to pass through the same." By this time, Indian land treaties had been made, reservations had been established, and the Black Hills were to be forever Indian territory. This was because the white man considered them to be worthless.

But by 1872 miners were disregarding the terms of the treaty and hunting for gold in the Black Hills. Paha Sapa, or the Black Hills, were considered by the Indians to be the center of the world, the place of spirits and holy matters. They were also a place where warriors went to pray to the Great Spirit and await visions. The violation of the treaty rights infuriated the Indians, and when they discovered prospectors on their sacred lands, they often killed them or chased them away. The gold-hungry prospectors demanded government

THE TRANSCONTINENTAL RAILROAD,
COMPLETED IN 1869, CUT ACROSS THE
PLAINS. THIS PAINTING SHOWS A GROUP
OF CHEYENNE LED BY TALL BULL
TEARING UP THE TRACKS,
AFTER ATTACKING A SECTION CREW
EARLIER IN THE DAY.

protection, and without consent from the Indians, troops were sent into the area.

More than one thousand mounted soldiers of the Seventh Cavalry under General George A. Custer crossed the Plains to the Black Hills. This did little to endear the white man to the Indians, and as Dee Brown says in *Bury My Heart at Wounded Knee*, "they were angry as hornets over the invasion of Paha Sapa...."

Finally, white commissioners attempted to persuade the Indians to sell the Black Hills outright for $6 million or to accept $400,000 yearly for mineral rights. Indian leaders met together and rejected both offers. The bureaucrats then returned to Washington and recommended to Congress that Indian wishes be disregarded and that the Indians be paid a "fair equivalent of the value of the Hills." In the end the intransigence of both sides would bring about a stunning defeat of Custer's troops at the Little Bighorn and the end of freedom for Northern Plains Indians as a result of the army massacre of Indians at Wounded Knee.

In December of 1875 the commissioner of Indian affairs in Washington ordered all Indians who were off the reservation to report to their agencies (headquarters for white officials on the reservations) by the end of January or a "military force would be sent to compel them." But by January 31, 1876, bad blizzards, heavy snows, and severe cold made travel across the Plains very difficult, particularly by horse and travois. It was impossible for the Indians to meet the deadline.

In February the War Department ordered operations against the recalcitrant Sioux, including the bands of the Hunkpapa Sioux of Sitting Bull and Crazy Horse's Oglala. The next day General Philip Sheridan commanded Generals Crook and Terry to prepare for military operations in the area of the headwaters of the Powder, Tongue, Rosebud, and Bighorn rivers.

On March 17 General Crook's forces attacked a group of Northern Cheyenne and Oglala Sioux who were camped on the Powder River, where they had gone to hunt for buffalo and antelope. It was not a war camp. They had many women and children with them. Wooden Leg, a young Cheyenne brave, said in his autobiography: "Old people tottered and hobbled away to get out of reach of the bullets singing among the lodges. Braves seized whatever weapons they had and tried to meet the attack. . . . From a distance we saw the destruction of our village. Our tepees were burned with everything in them. I had nothing left but the clothing I had on." The following spring the Sioux who had escaped to the hills came out of hiding and were led by Crazy Horse in a decisive victory over General Crook in the Battle of the Rosebud.

Another skirmish on the Rosebud River between Indians and Bluecoats ended more favorably for the Cheyenne and Sioux. After this fight the Indians decided to move west to the valley of the Little Bighorn. By this time the Indian encampment of Oglala Sioux and Cheyenne numbered some ten thousand people, including four thousand warriors. Nearby toward the south was a Hunkpapa camp, and near it, Blackfoot Sioux. Below them were the Sans Arc, Miniconjou, and additional Oglala and Brulé Sioux. At the north end were the Cheyenne. The Hunkpapa's chief, Sitting Bull, assumed authority over all the combined camps. By June 24 they heard that Longhair Custer (General Custer) was near the Rosebud, and by the next day their scouts reported that Custer's forces were marching toward the Little Bighorn.

The Crow, traditional enemies of the Cheyenne and generally friendly to the whites, were employed as scouts by Custer's troops. Many Crow also lost their lives on the Little Bighorn battlefield.

The battle that followed, known variously as Custer's Last Stand or the Battle of the Little Bighorn, ended in annihilation of the white Bluecoats. It was the Indians' greatest victory — and their last.

HOW THE WEST WAS LOST

Following the Custer battle in 1876 both Sioux and Cheyenne were constantly pursued and attacked by United States government troops. Sitting Bull and some of his followers managed to escape to Canada and were given temporary refuge by the Canadian government as long as they kept their promise not to cross the border to fight the Americans. The Powder River country and the Black Hills were gone forever as Indian lands. The United States government also sliced off another fifty-mile strip adjoining the Black Hills. There was then pressure to move all the Teton Sioux south to Indian Territory (now Oklahoma), but the persistence of Red Cloud and Spotted Tail prevailed. Red Cloud's Oglala were settled at Pine Ridge, South Dakota. Spotted Tail's people settled on the Little White River. The agency was named Rosebud. Four other agencies were established for remaining Sioux tribes —

Lower Brulé, Crow Creek, Cheyenne River, and Standing Rock.

Meanwhile, Sitting Bull's Canadian exile was turning into disaster. The Canadian government refused to give him a reservation, and rather than submit to starvation, he led his followers back to the United States and surrendered at Fort Buford, North Dakota on July 19, 1881.

In the eight years that followed (during which Sitting Bull was set free and allowed to live on the reservation at Standing Rock), a great deal of skulduggery was being planned in Washington. A Washington commission proposed to divide the great Sioux reservation into six smaller ones, leaving nine million acres open for white settlement. The Indians were offered fifty cents an acre for the land. However, the Indians refused to sign and the three-fourths majority needed was not obtained. The frustrated commissioners returned to Washington and recommended the land be taken without the consent of the Indians. But by August of 1889 the Indians had finally been coerced into signing, and the great Sioux reservation was broken up.

This, however, was not the only tragedy that would involve the Sioux. The Paiute, or Fish Eaters, lived near Pyramid Lake in Nevada. One of their number claimed to be the Messiah, Christ returned to earth as an Indian. He preached that Indians must dance a "Ghost Dance." Short Bull (Sitting Bull's brother-in-law) and a Miniconjou named Kicking Bear traveled with a group of Sioux by train to Nevada and finally met the Messiah at the Paiute Agency at Walker Lake. The Paiute Messiah, Wovoka, taught that if the Indians danced the Ghost Dance, dead Indians would be returned to earth.

"ALL INDIANS MUST DANCE, EVERYWHERE...."
AS THE GHOST DANCE SPREAD
THROUGHOUT THE SIOUX RESERVATIONS,
WHITE AGENTS BECAME FRIGHTENED,
SEEING IT AS A SIGN OF REBELLION.

Great herds of game would return, and the whites would be destroyed in a great flood. His teachings have been preserved in his own words:

All Indians must dance, everywhere, keep on dancing. Pretty soon in next spring Great Spirit come. He bring back all game of every kind. The game be thick everywhere. All dead Indians come back and live again. They all be strong just like young men, be young again. Old blind Indian see again and get young and have fine time. When Great Spirit comes this way, then all the Indians go to mountains high up away from whites. Whites can't hurt Indians then. Then while Indians way up high, big flood comes like water and all white people die, get drowned. After that, water go away and then nobody but Indians everywhere and game all kinds thick. Then medicine man tell Indians to send word to all Indians to keep dancing and the good time will come. Indians who don't dance, who don't believe in this word, will grow little, just about a foot high, and stay that way. Some of them will be turned into wood and be burned in fire.

Not all Indians believed the Messiah. Sitting Bull, for one, did not believe dead men could be brought back to life, but he did not object to his people dancing the Ghost Dance. Soon the dancing was common throughout the Sioux reservation. White agents generally became frightened, although some saw no harm in the Ghost Dance.

One frightened agent was James McLaughlin at Standing Rock. He was jealous and suspicious of Sitting Bull's power and ordered Sitting Bull arrested. On December 15, 1890,

Sitting Bull refused to go peacefully with the officers and was shot and killed by agency police, along with his seventeen-year-old son, Crowfoot, and six other members of his tribe.

Many of Sitting Bull's Hunkpapa fled to Red Cloud's camp at Pine Ridge. Some went to the Miniconjou camp near Cherry Creek. The War Department then ordered the imprisonment of Big Foot, leader of the Miniconjou. Hoping for protection from Red Cloud, Big Foot started his people toward Pine Ridge. En route he got pneumonia and was finally confronted by Major Samuel Whitside of the Seventh U.S. Cavalry. Big Foot and his followers were ordered to camp at Wounded Knee.

At Wounded Knee the Indians numbered 120 men and 230 women and children. They were ordered to disarm, and their tepees were searched for weapons. Only two rifles were found. A deaf young Miniconjou named Black Coyote objected to giving up his new Winchester rifle. However, according to eyewitness accounts, he was going to surrender the gun when he was grabbed by troops. As he was grabbed and spun around, the gun went off. Immediately the soldiers returned fire and the massacre was in full swing. The Indians tried to flee. At that point big Hotchkiss guns on the hill opened up on them, according to author Dee Brown, "firing almost a shell a second, raking the Indian camp, shredding the tepees with flying shrapnel, killing men, women and children." One Indian woman, Louise Weasel Bear, said, "We tried to run but they shot us like we were a buffalo."

At the end of the massacre Big Foot and more than half of his people were dead or wounded. In the words of Red Cloud: "We heard that soldiers were coming. We did not fear.

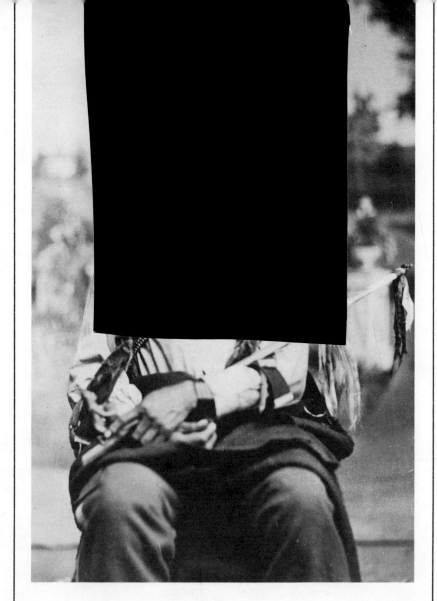

SITTING BULL

THE BATTLEFIELD AT WOUNDED KNEE,
AFTER THE MASSACRE

We hoped we could tell them our troubles and get help. A white man said the soldiers meant to kill us. We did not believe it."

Some estimate that 300 of the original 350 Indians died. The wounded Sioux, 4 men and 47 women and children, were taken in wagons by a detail of soldiers to Pine Ridge.

With this incident the back of Indian rights was broken. The Indian sentiment is best summed up by Black Elk, an Oglala Sioux, who said:

> I did not know then how much was ended. When I look back now, from this high hill of my old age, I can still see the butchered women and children lying heaped and scattered all along the crooked gulch as plain as when I saw them with eyes still young. And I can see that something else died there, in the bloody mud, and was buried in the blizzard. A people's dream died there. It was a beautiful dream . . . the nation's hoop is broken and scattered. There is no center any longer, and the sacred tree is dead.

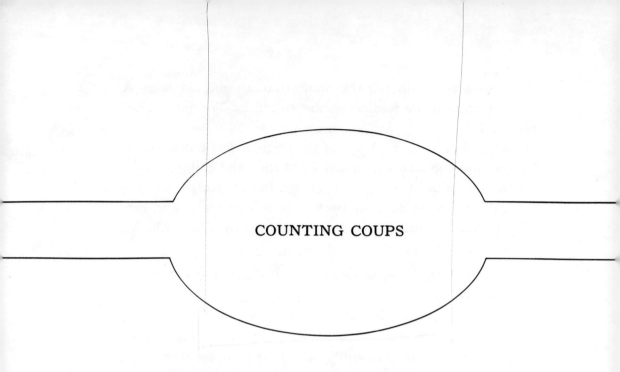

COUNTING COUPS

One custom common to all Plains Indian tribes was "counting coups." The term came from the French Canadian word *coup*, which means "blow or stroke," and was used to designate a formal token of victory in battle. Counting coups was important to becoming a respected hunter and warrior. In ceremonial parades and functions an ornamented whip or rod was sometimes carried and used as a coup stick to show off a man's successful exploits, as one today wears medals.

Credit for a coup during battle was taken for three brave deeds — killing an enemy, scalping an enemy, or being the first person to strike an enemy physically either alive or dead. Each one of these coups entitled a man to rank as a warrior and to recount the exploit in public. Some tribes allowed three coups to be counted by three different persons on the body of the same enemy. Other tribes allowed four.

To be first to touch the enemy was the bravest deed of all. This coup might be made with whatever was most convenient, even with the naked hand. The simple touch scored the victory. Among the Cheyenne it was a point of bravery for a single warrior to rush the enemy and strike him with a quirt (a whip made of braided rawhide) or gun butt before attempting to fire. This meant the warrior was duly risking his own life.

Stealing a horse from a hostile camp also carried the right to count coups, as did striking the tepee of an enemy in a charge. The latter entitled the warrior to reproduce the tepee's particular design on his next new tepee and to perpetuate the pattern in his family. In this way he was said to have "captured" the tepee. Warriors who had made coups of distinguished bravery such as striking an enemy within his own tepee or behind breastworks were selected to preside over the dedication of a new tepee.

The famous Sioux warrior Red Cloud claimed he had counted coups eighty times. A famous Crow chief had counted so many coups that he was named Plenty Coups. He counted his first coup at the age of nine when, on foot, he struck a wounded buffalo bull with his bow.

SIGNS OF THE TIMES

The Plains Indians developed a unique system of communication. This was the sign language. By using hand signs, all the tribes could understand each other regardless of the language they spoke. It was also a silent language, so there was no danger of alerting an enemy. When white trappers, traders, explorers, and settlers arrived in Indian country, many learned the sign language. It was easier for white people than complicated Indian languages.

Practiced speakers of sign language could communicate by sign as quickly as they could orally. In some ways the sign language is very poetic. The signs in every case are founded on some solid or symbolic characteristic.

Here are some sign language movements:

MAN. Put your hand (palm down) in front of you. Raise

COMMUNICATING THROUGH SIGN LANGUAGE

your index finger and move your hand back and up toward you.

WOMAN. Put your hand at the side of your head, fingers toward the hair. Make a downward sweeping movement as if you were combing your hair.

WHITE MAN. Draw your index finger across your forehead, or grasp your forehead with your thumb and index finger. This sign shows the white man as a hat wearer.

INDIAN. Rub the back of your left hand or cheek with the palm of the right. This indicates a person whose skin is of the same color. (A white person may use this sign when speaking of another white.)

TEPEE. Bring both index fingers together like an upside down V.

BUFFALO. Crook the index finger at the side of the head to resemble a horn.

DOG. Spread first and second fingers apart and draw the hand across in front of your body. This sign expresses the travois, once pulled by a dog when it was used as a beast of burden.

SLEEPING. Incline the head to one side with the palm of the hand held just below. Days or nights are counted by sleeps. To indicate days, make the sign for sleep and then count on your fingers the number of days you wish to show.

COLD. Clench your hands in front of your body and make a shivering motion. The years may be counted by using this sign, plus counting on your fingers.

A QUESTION. The hand palm up, fingers apart, and wrist turned quickly. A slow turning of the wrist means "maybe."

Putting some of these signs together, you can ask a question. For example, "How old are you?"

1. Point finger at subject — You.
2. Cold sign — Winters — Years.
3. Counting sign — Number.
4. Question sign — How many?

Each tribe had various signs to indicate another tribe. For example, a sign for the Blackfeet was to pass a flat hand over the outside edge of the right foot (from the heel to beyond the toe) as if brushing off dust.

A Sioux sign for Cheyenne Indians was to make a motion as though sawing through the middle of the left forearm with the edge of the right hand held thumb up. This sign is made at the left side of the body. The same sign is used to indicate a saw. The Cheyenne were known by the Sioux as the "Saws."

A much-used sign for Sioux Indians was to pass the flat right hand, palm down, from left to right across the throat. Some of the tribes referred to the Sioux as "Cutthroats."

When Indians were too far away from each other to see hand signals, they used a sort of telegraphic communication system of their own design — smoke signals. Smoke signals were often used to warn of danger or to indicate the presence of game.

A fire was built on a high point. It was usually made of damp grass, weeds, cedar tops, or another material that would burn slowly and throw out dense smoke. Once lit, it was allowed to burn to attract attention. The signaler then proceeded with the message by throwing a blanket over the smoldering pile and withdrawing it, allowing a single puff of smoke to ascend. This procedure was repeated time and again until, by the number and length of the puffs, the watchers in the faraway camp knew whether buffalo or enemies had been discovered. Regular camping places all had their predetermined signal stations.

The Indians also had a "discovery" signal, which was carried out on horseback. The signaler rode in a circle because this movement could be seen from any direction. Once he noticed increased activity in the receiving camp, he made a specific signal for either buffalo or enemy. For buffalo he held an open blanket at two corners, with his arms outstretched above his head, and gracefully brought the blanket down toward the ground. The "enemy" signal was made by confused and rapid riding back and forth. It could also be made by waving an outstretched blanket rapidly above the head. An alarm was signaled by throwing the blanket into the air several times in quick succession. When the coast was clear, an open blanket was gently waved from side to side in front of the body.

Drums were also used in signaling. Trail marks were another means of communication, indicating the passing of a traveler or party or the occurrence of a notable incident. These varied from a simple bent twig or pile of stones to a charred tree or elaborate pictograph set in a conspicuous place.

INDIAN ORATORS

The silent, inarticulate Indian is a false stereotype, for there have been many great orators, poets, and writers among the Indian people. Many of the speeches of famous Indian leaders have been preserved.

Spotted Tail, a brilliant Sioux leader who was controversial among his own people because of his negotiations with the whites, spoke at a council meeting of Indians and whites in 1877. His speech shows much of the basic Indian philosophy and also a willingness to live in peace and harmony with the whites. He said:

My friends, your people have both intellect and heart; you use these to consider in what way you can do the best to live. My people, who are here before you, are pre-

SPOTTED TAIL, PHOTOGRAPHED IN 1872

cisely the same. I see that my friends before me are men of age and dignity, and men of that kind have good judgment and consider well what they do. I infer from that, that you are here to consider what shall be good for my people for a long time to come. I think each of you has selected somewhere a good piece of land for himself with the intention to live on it, that he may there raise his children. My people are not different. We also live upon the earth and upon the things that come to them from above. We have the same thoughts and desires in that respect that the white people have. This is the country where they were born, where they have acquired all their property, their children and their horses. You have come here to buy this country of us; and it would be well if you would come with the goods you propose to give us, and to put them out of your hand so we can see the good price you propose to pay for it. Then our hearts would be glad.

My friends, when you go back to the Great Father [President of the United States], I want you to tell him to send us goods; send us yokes and oxen, and give us wagons so we can earn money by hauling goods from the railroads. This seems to be a very hard day; half of our country is at war, and we have come upon very difficult times. This war did not spring up here in our land. It was brought upon us by the children of the Great Father, who came to take our land from us without price, and who do many evil things; the Great Father and his children are to blame for this trouble. We have here a great storehouse, and when our people become displeased with our provisions and have gone North to hunt, the children of the Great Father are fighting them. It has been our wish to live here peaceably, but the Great Father has filled it with soldiers who think only of our death. Some of our people who have gone from here in order that they may have a change, and others have been attacked by the soldiers from other directions; and now that they are willing to come back, the soldiers stand between them and keep them from coming home. It seems to me there is a better way than this. When people come to trouble it is better for both parties to come together without arms, to talk it over, and find some peaceful way to settle.

As Crazy Horse lay dying, mortally wounded by the thrust of a bayonet, his dying words to Indian Agent Jesse M. Lee were:

My friend, I do not blame you for this. Had I listened to you this trouble would not have happened to me. I was not hostile to the white men. Sometimes my young men would attack the Indians who were their enemies and took their ponies. They did it in return.

We had buffalo for food, and their hides for clothing and for our teepees. We preferred hunting to a life of idleness on the reservation, where we were driven against our will. At times we did not get enough to eat, and we were not allowed to leave the reservation to hunt.

We preferred our own way of living. We were no expense to the government. All we wanted was peace and to be left alone. Soldiers were sent out in the winter, who destroyed our villages.

Then "Long Hair" [Custer] came in the same way. They say we massacred him, but he would have done the same thing to us had we not defended ourselves and fought to the last. Our first impulse was to escape with our squaws and papooses, but we were so hemmed in that we had to fight.

After that I went up on the Tongue River with a few of my people and lived in peace. But the government would not let me alone. Finally, I came back to the Red Cloud Agency. Yet I was not allowed to remain quiet.

I was tired of fighting. I went to the Spotted Tail Agency and asked that chief and his agent to let me live there in peace. I came here with the agent [Lee] to talk with the Big White Chief but was not given a chance. They tried to confine me. I tried to escape, and a soldier ran his bayonet into me.

I have spoken.

RESERVATION LIFE TODAY

Plains Indian life today is still filled with hardship — but of a different sort than the hardships of the eighteenth and early nineteenth centuries. Today most Plains Indians live on reservations (lands designated for Indian use), although some do live in urban centers throughout the United States.

Many whites believe that Indians should assimilate themselves into white society by adopting its values and customs, and there are Indians who have successfully made this transition. But, increasingly, the Indian population, particularly the young people, are resisting this attempt to make them over in the image of white people.

To many Indians the call for assimilation is viewed suspiciously as an attempt to separate them from their Indian identity and as an excuse for taking the rest of their lands. Consequently there is a concerted effort today by young Indians to cling to many of their traditional beliefs and ways of life. But this does not mean that these Indians are satisfied with their standard of living. They have the same material needs and aspirations as whites. They simply do not believe they must live as whites to better their circumstances.

In 1972 Indians took over the Bureau of Indian Affairs in Washington and in February 1973 they occupied the town of Wounded Knee, South Dakota. To understand both these occurrences, it is best to look at Indian-white relations chronologically:

1879 — A lower court ruled that an individual Indian has the same constitutional rights as a non-Indian.

1880 — Federal jurisdiction on Indian reservations was established for major crimes such as murder, rape, and burglary.

Indian police forces were formed by the Bureau of Indian Affairs, which was first organized in 1834 under the War Department and in 1849 transferred to the Department of the Interior.

1924 — All Indians became citizens, whether they wanted to or not. This meant that their individual cash allotments from the government became taxable and lands could be seized for unpaid taxes.

1934 — The Indian Reorganization Act created the present form of tribal government. (See chart on following page.) The act was approved because many Indian traditionalists protested by boycotting the vote on the referendum.

SECRETARY OF INTERIOR

COMMISSIONER OF INDIAN AFFAIRS,
BUREAU OF INDIAN AFFAIRS

AREA DIRECTOR, BUREAU OF INDIAN AFFAIRS

RESERVATION SUPERINTENDENT,
BUREAU OF INDIAN AFFAIRS

PRESIDENT OR CHAIRMAN

TREASURER

VICE-PRESIDENT

SECRETARY

TRIBAL COUNCILMAN

Notes: (1) Without the approval of the Bureau of Indian Affairs, no act of tribal government except taxation of tribal members can be performed. (2) The people of each district elect one tribal councilman.

1942 — Five hundred square miles of the Pine Ridge (Sioux) Reservation were seized by the government as a practice bombing range.

1944 — The National Congress of American Indians was formed to act as a lobbying group in Washington for Indian rights and benefits.

By the 1950s a government relocation policy moved many Indians to cities and produced Indian slums and urban poverty pockets all over the West Coast and Midwest.

1961 — The National Indian Youth Council was formed in New Mexico. It was the first all-Indian youth group to protest and demonstrate for Indian rights.

1968 — The American Indian Movement (AIM) was organized in Minneapolis by two Chippewa, Dennis Banks and George Mitchell. It is built around total Indian self-determination. According to Russell Means, an Oglala Sioux and leader of AIM, AIM leaders agree that "it is the responsibility of the Indian people themselves to change realities around them, when these realities are repressive and oppressive. We are simply doing those things that all Indians agree should be done in a way that will be effective." AIM members are activists, mostly young, although older men and women also support the movement. Not all Indian leaders are sympathetic to AIM, a fact that Russell Means freely admits when he says, "AIM has never claimed to be representatives of all the Indian people — we represent the facts of Indian life."

1969 — A San Francisco group called Indians of All Tribes seized Alcatraz Island in an attempt to dramatize Indian problems and set up a cultural center. It was an ambitious attempt but doomed to failure as authorities cut off water and other essential services.

1972 — On the eve of the presidential election, many hundreds of Indians — young and old, men, women, and children from reservation lands and urban areas — formed the Trail of Broken Treaties in a march on Washington. They demanded redress against wrongs such as broken treaties, poverty, bad housing, and poor schooling. Because government leaders chose not to negotiate with the Indians, the resulting Indian frustration ended in a seizure of the Bureau of Indian Affairs building in Washington.

1973 — On February 27, AIM leaders, including Dennis Banks and Russell Means, captured the small town of Wounded Knee at gunpoint to dramatize poverty and alleged corruption and oppression at Pine Ridge Reservation. According to Robert Burnette, Tribal Chairman of the Rosebud Sioux Reservation, the causes of the Wounded Knee takeover were "leasing arrangements that cheated Indians out of the income on their lands, crooked trading posts, the dictatorial tribal councils and the nepotism that kept the full bloods out of the only jobs available, while the Chairmen hired their friends and relatives."

In the end many Indians were brought to trial in Min-

DURING THE TAKEOVER OF THE BUREAU
OF INDIAN AFFAIRS IN 1972, A GROUP OF
DEMONSTRATORS GUARDS THE ENTRANCE.

neapolis, but Federal Judge Fred Nichol, after many weeks of testimony, dismissed all the charges against the defendants due to the misconduct of the United States government, including evidence of lying by agents of the Federal Bureau of Investigation.

Until the white people's promises to the Indians are kept, and the prejudice and antagonism toward the Indian (particularly in areas bordering large Indian populations) are erased and replaced by understanding and compassion, there is likely to be continued trouble between Indian activists and government bureaucrats. But the future is not hopeless. Many self-help programs have been initiated on Indian reservations. Small industries have been established, and even some ski resorts and motels are Indian owned and operated. Today's young Indians are working hard to preserve their traditions, to achieve education, to better their health, and to perpetuate their culture.

FOR FURTHER READING

Bear, Luther Standing. *My People the Sioux.* Lincoln, Neb. University of Nebraska Press, 1975.

Black Elk. *Sacred Pipe: Black Elk's Account of the Seven Rites of the Oglala Sioux.* Joseph E. Brown, ed. Norman, Okla.: University of Oklahoma Press, 1970.

Blish, Helen H., and Bad Heart Bull, Amos. *A Pictographic History of the Oglala Sioux.* Lincoln, Neb.: University of Nebraska Press, 1967.

Brown, Dee. *Bury My Heart at Wounded Knee: An Indian History of the American West.* New York: Holt, Rinehart & Winston, 1971.

Catlin, George. *Letters & Notes on the Manners, Customs & Conditions of the North American Indians.* 2 vols. New York: Dover, 1973.

Jacobson, Daniel. *The Hunters.* New York: Franklin Watts, 1974.

Levenson, Dorothy. *Homesteaders and Indians.* (A First Book.) New York: Franklin Watts, 1971.

Linderman, Frank B. *Plenty-Coups, Chief of the Crows.* New York: John Day, 1972.

Sheppard, Sally. *Indians of the Eastern Woodlands.* (A First Book.) New York: Franklin Watts, 1975.

Yellow Robe, Rosebud. *An Album of the American Indian.* New York: Franklin Watts, 1969.

INDEX

Absaroka, 10
Agencies, Indian, 58–59
Alcatraz Island, seizure of, 82
American Indian Movement, 81, 82
Amos Bad Heart Bull, 45
Amusements, 49, 51
Apaches, 23
Arapaho, 2
Art, 44–45, 47
Asia, humans from, 2
Assiniboine, 25

Bands, 3, 5, 7–8, 13–14, 45
Banks, Dennis, 81, 82
Battle of Little Bighorn, 55–57
    painting of, 45, 47
Battle of the Rosebud, 56
Battles, 45, 47, 53, 55–57
Beadwork, 44–45
Bering Strait, 2
Big Foot, 62
Black Coyote, 62

Black Elk, quoted, 65
Black Hills, 7, 53, 55, 58
Blackfeet, 13–14, 25, 47, 56, 71
Blackfoot Confederacy, 2, 13–14
Brown, Dee, 55, 62
Brulé, 5, 37, 56
Buffalo, 11, 26–28, 30, 31, 37, 45, 52, 70,
    72
Bureau of Indian Affairs, 79, 80, 82
Burnette, Robert, 82
Bury My Heart at Wounded Knee
    (Brown), 55

Canada, 2, 58, 59
Catlin, George, 7, 10, 28
Cheyenne, 2, 6–8, 47, 49, 51, 56, 58, 67, 71
Clans, 3, 10–11
Climate, 1–2, 18
Clothing, 15, 17, 26, 44–45
Clowns, 34
Comanche, 2, 23
Confederacy. *See* Nation

Coups, counting of, 66–67
Crazy Horse, 52, 55–56, 76–77
Cree, 25
Crook, General George, 56
Crow, 2, 3, 10–11, 13, 17, 40–41, 57
Crowfoot, 62
Custer, General George, 45, 47, 55–57, 77

Dakota dialect, 5
Dakota Sioux, legend of, 42–43
Dancing, 31, 34, 36–39, 48, 59, 61
Dialects, 5
Dreams, 33–34, 41
Drums, for signaling, 72

Federal Bureau of Investigation, 84
Food, 2, 6–7, 18, 26
Forests, 1–2
Fort Buford, 59

Games. See Amusements
Ghost Dance, 59, 61
Gold, hunt for, 53, 55
Great Father, 75–76
Great Spirit, 37, 43, 61
Grinnell, George Bird, 30
Guns, Blackfeet and, 25

Hair, 10, 17
Headdresses, 17
High Bull, painting by, 47
History, tribal, painting of, 45
Horses, 7, 8, 21–23, 25, 27–28, 30, 45, 67, 72
Housing, 18, 26
Humans, first, in North America, 2
Hunkpapa, 5, 55–56, 62
Hunting, 11, 14, 18, 52
    of buffalo, 11, 27–28, 30, 31

Indian Reorganization Act, 79
Indian Territory, 58
Indians of All Tribes, 82

Kainah, 13

Kicking Bear, 59
Kiowa, 2

Lakota dialect, 5
Land, 30, 52–53, 55, 58, 59, 75
Lee, Jesse M., 76–77
Legends, 40–43
Linderman, Frank B., 11, 13
Little White River, 58
Louise Weasel Bear, 62
Luther Standing Bear, 37–39

McLaughlin, James, 61
Mdewakanton, 5
Means, Russell, 81, 82
Messiah, Indian, 59, 61
Migrations, prehistoric, 2
Miniconjou, 5, 56, 59, 62
Mitchell, George, 81
Montana, 1, 59
Mountain Crow, 10
Mountains, and climate, 1–2
Museum of the American Indian, New York, 47
Music, 47–48
Myths, 40–43

Nakota dialect, 5
Nation, of Indians, 3
National Congress of American Indians, 81
National Indian Youth Council, 81
Nez Percé, 2
Nichol, Judge Fred, 82
Northern Plains, 2, 23, 25

Oceti Sakowin, 5
Oglala, 5, 45, 52, 55–56, 58, 65
Oklahoma, 58
Osage, 7

Paha Sapa. See Black Hills
Painting, 45, 47
Paiute, 59
Parfleches, 26–27

Pawnee, 2
Phratries, 11
*Pictographic History of the Oglala Sioux,
   A,* 45
Piegan, 13
Pine Ridge, 58, 62, 65, 81, 82
Pipe, smoking of, 42–43, 53
Plains, grassy, 1, 2
Plains Indians, present life of, 78–82,
   84
Plenty Coups, 11, 67
Ponca, 2
Powder River, 56, 58
Pueblo Indians, 23

Quillwork, 44

Red Cloud, 58, 62, 67
Red Cloud Agency, 77
Red Crane, 47
Religion, 31, 33–34, 36–39
River Crow, 10
Rocky Mountains, 1–2
Rosebud Reservation, 58, 82
Rosebud River, battle of, 56

Sans Arc, 5, 56
Santee, 5
Seven Council Fires, 5, 7
Sheridan, General Philip, 25, 56
Shoshoni, and Blackfeet, 23, 25
Sign language, 68, 70–71
Signals, 71–72
Sihasapa, 5
Siksika, 13
Sioux, 2, 5–7, 34, 36–39, 41–42, 55–59,
   61–62, 65, 71
Sisseton, 5
Sitting Bull, 55, 56, 58, 59, 61, 62
Short Bull, 59
Smoke signals, 71–72
South Dakota, 7, 53, 58

Spanish, and horses, 23
Spotted Tail, 58, 73, 75–76
Spotted Tail Agency, 77
Suh tai, 6
Sun Dance, 14, 34, 36–39
Sweat Lodge Ceremony, 33

Tashunka Witko. *See* Crazy Horse
Tepees, 18, 21, 22, 26, 67, 70
Terry, General Alfred H., 56
Teton, 5, 58
Trail marks, as signals, 72
Trail of Broken Treaties, 82
Tribes, 3, 5, 71, 80
Tsis tsis tas, 6
Two Kettle, 5
Two Leggings, 40

United States government, and Indians,
   53, 55–59, 61, 62, 65, 79–82, 84
Ute, and horses, 23
Utensils, 26, 44

Wahpekute, 5
Wahpeton, 5
Wakan Tanka. *See* Great Spirit
Walker Lake, agency at, 59
Warrior societies, 7–8, 14
Whites, Indians and, 30, 52–53, 55, 61–
   62, 65, 73, 75–76, 78, 79–84
Whitside, Major Samuel, 62
Wigwam, 18–21
   See also Tepees
Winchester repeater, 30
Women, 3, 5, 8, 11, 15, 21, 70
   and arts, 44–45
Wooden Leg, quoted, 56
Wounded Knee, 55, 62, 65, 79, 82
Wovoka, 59

Yankton, 5
Yanktonai, 5